"Mindfulness in 5 Minutes"

Easy mindfulness exercises that can be done anywhere, anytime

ROHAN MODY

Mindfulness in 5 minutes   Micro Series

Copyright © 2024 ROHAN MODY.
All rights reserved. This book or any portion thereof may not be reproduced or used in any manner whatsoever without the express written permission of the publisher except for the use of brief quotations in a book review.
Published by Rohan Mody, in India.
First Published, September 2024.
Publisher – KINDLE DIRECT PUBLISHING

SYNOPSIS

Easy mindfulness exercises that can be done anywhere, anytime. This book provides practical techniques to integrate mindfulness into your daily routine, helping you find calm and clarity in just five minutes a day.

INTRODUCTION

Mindfulness doesn't have to be an elaborate practice requiring hours of meditation or a quiet retreat. In our fast-paced world, finding moments of calm can seem impossible, but with the right techniques, you can cultivate mindfulness in just five minutes a day. This book will equip you with simple, actionable exercises that fit seamlessly into your lifestyle, allowing you to pause, breathe, and reconnect with the present moment, no matter where you are.

Mindfulness in 5 minutes　　　Micro Series

- Micro Self-Improvement Series –
Minimal Bite-sized self-improvement strategies that are easy to implement on a daily basis.

Crafted for individuals who like to
Read less, Do More!

Each book in the series focuses on one area of personal growth, offering quick, actionable tips for improvement.

TABLE OF CONTENTS :

Chapter 1: The Power of Five Minutes 7

Chapter 2: Breathing Techniques for Instant Calm 10

Chapter 3: Mindful Observation 13

Chapter 4: Mindful Movement 16

Chapter 5: Mindfulness in Daily Activities 19

Chapter 6: Mindfulness and Technology 22

Chapter 7: The Power of Gratitude in Mindfulness 25

Chapter 8: Creating Your Mindfulness Routine 28

Chapter 9: Mindfulness in Everyday Activities 31

Chapter 10: Overcoming Mindfulness Challenges 34

Chapter 11: Mindfulness for Stress Management 37

Chapter 12: Integrating Mindfulness into Your Lifestyle 39

Conclusion: Your Mindful Journey Begins Now 42

What's Your Next Mindful Moment? 43

Mindfulness in 5 minutes   Micro Series

Chapter 1: The Power of Five Minutes

Understanding Mindfulness

Mindfulness is the practice of being present and fully engaged with the moment. It's about observing your thoughts and feelings without judgment. While it may sound simple, incorporating mindfulness into your daily life can significantly enhance your well-being and reduce stress.

Why Five Minutes?

Five minutes might not seem like much, but it's enough time to shift your focus, reset your mind, and cultivate awareness. Here's why these brief practices can be powerful:

1. Accessibility: Anyone can spare five minutes, making mindfulness more approachable and sustainable.
2. Immediate Impact: Short practices provide quick relief from stress and anxiety, promoting a sense of calm that can last throughout the day.
3. Consistency: Small, regular practices build a habit. The more you engage in mindfulness, the more natural it becomes.

Action Step: Commit to Your Five Minutes

- Choose a Time: Select a specific time each day to practice mindfulness—morning, lunch break, or before bed. Consistency is key.
- Find Your Space: Identify a place where you can practice without interruptions. It could be your bedroom, office, or even a quiet corner in a café.
- Set an Intention: Before you begin, set a clear intention for your practice. It could be to cultivate calmness, focus, or self-compassion.

Example Exercise: The 5-Minute Breathing Space

1. Get Comfortable: Sit or stand in a comfortable position. Close your eyes if you feel comfortable doing so.
2. Breathe Naturally: Begin to notice your breath without trying to change it. Feel the air entering and leaving your body.
3. Acknowledge Your Thoughts: Recognize any thoughts that arise. Simply

observe them without judgment—let them pass like clouds in the sky.

4. Deepen Your Breath: After a minute, start taking deeper breaths. Inhale through your nose, filling your lungs, and exhale through your mouth.

5. Return to the Present: Gradually bring your awareness back to your surroundings. Open your eyes, stretch, and take a moment before returning to your day.

Reflect on Your Experience

After your practice, take a moment to reflect. How do you feel? What thoughts or sensations did you notice? This reflection reinforces the benefits of mindfulness and encourages you to continue.

Chapter Summary

Incorporating mindfulness into your life doesn't require hours of practice—just five minutes a day can make a significant difference. By committing to regular, short mindfulness exercises, you'll create a lasting habit that enhances your overall well-being.

Chapter 2: Breathing Techniques for Instant Calm

The Breath as Your Anchor

One of the simplest yet most effective tools for mindfulness is your breath. It's always with you, available to help you anchor your thoughts and bring you back to the present moment. Learning to harness the power of your breath can help you manage stress, reduce anxiety, and cultivate a sense of peace.

Understanding Breath Awareness

Breath awareness involves focusing your attention on your breathing patterns. This practice can ground you, providing clarity and focus in moments of distraction or stress. Here's how it works:

1.	Reduces Stress: Focusing on your breath helps calm the mind and reduces the body's stress response.
2.	Increases Awareness: It trains your mind to notice when it wanders, gently guiding it back to the present.
3.	Promotes Relaxation: Deep, mindful breathing activates the body's relaxation response, counteracting feelings of anxiety.

Action Step: Practice the 4-7-8 Breathing Technique

This technique, developed by Dr. Andrew Weil, promotes relaxation and reduces anxiety. Here's how to do it:

1.	Find a Comfortable Position: Sit or lie down in a quiet space where you won't be disturbed.
2.	Close Your Eyes: If you feel comfortable, close your eyes to eliminate distractions.
3.	Inhale Through Your Nose: Take a deep breath in through your nose for a count of 4.
4.	Hold Your Breath: Retain your breath for a count of 7.
5.	Exhale Slowly: Release your breath slowly through your mouth for a count of 8.
6.	Repeat: Complete this cycle for four breaths.

Reflection: Notice the Shift

After practicing the 4-7-8 technique, take a moment to reflect. What changes did you feel in your body and mind? Did you notice any shifts in your thoughts or emotions? This self-awareness deepens your mindfulness practice.

Example Exercise: Breath Counting

1. Sit Comfortably: Sit in a comfortable position with your back straight.
2. Breathe Naturally: Start with a few natural breaths to settle into the moment.
3. Count Your Breaths: As you breathe in, silently count "one." As you breathe out, count "two." Continue counting up to five, then start over.
4. Stay Focused: If your mind wanders, gently bring your focus back to counting your breaths.

Chapter Summary

Breathing techniques are powerful tools for cultivating mindfulness and reducing stress. By practicing the 4-7-8 breathing method or breath counting, you can develop a greater awareness of your breath and its calming effects.

Chapter 3: Mindful Observation

The Art of Observation

Mindful observation is about being fully present and engaged with your surroundings. It involves using your senses to experience the world around you without judgment. This practice helps ground you and enhances your appreciation for the present moment.

Why Mindful Observation Matters

1. Enhances Awareness: Engaging your senses helps anchor your thoughts and cultivates a deeper awareness of your environment.
2. Fosters Gratitude: Observing the beauty in everyday moments can increase feelings of gratitude and joy.

3.   Reduces Distractions: Focusing on your surroundings pulls you away from the distractions of your mind.

Action Step: The 5-Minute Observation Exercise

1.   Choose Your Environment: Find a place where you can sit quietly, whether it's indoors or outdoors.
2.   Set a Timer: Set a timer for five minutes to encourage focused observation.
3.   Engage Your Senses:
•   Sight: Look around you and notice the colors, shapes, and movements. What stands out?
•   Sound: Close your eyes and listen carefully. What sounds do you hear? Birds, traffic, voices?
•   Touch: If possible, feel the texture of an object nearby. What does it feel like?
•   Smell: Take a deep breath. What scents are present?
4.   Reflect: After five minutes, take a moment to reflect on your observations. How did this practice make you feel?

Example Exercise: Mindful Eating

1.   Choose a Snack: Pick a small snack to enjoy mindfully.
2.   Engage Your Senses: Before eating, observe the snack. Notice its color, texture, and shape.
3.   Take Small Bites: As you eat, chew slowly and savor each bite. Pay attention to the flavour's and how they change.

4.   Reflect on the Experience: After you finish, reflect on how the mindful eating experience felt compared to your usual way of eating.

Chapter Summary

Mindful observation invites you to engage fully with the present moment using your senses. By practicing mindful observation and mindful eating, you cultivate awareness and appreciation for the world around you, enhancing your overall mindfulness practice.

Chapter 4: Mindful Movement

Embracing Movement with Awareness

Mindful movement is about integrating mindfulness into physical activities. Whether you're walking, stretching, or exercising, you can cultivate mindfulness by paying attention to your body's movements and sensations. This practice not only enhances your physical health but also connects your mind and body.

The Benefits of Mindful Movement

1. Improves Physical Awareness: By focusing on how your body feels as you move, you enhance your awareness of physical sensations and improve coordination.
2. Reduces Stress: Engaging in mindful movement can help release built-up tension in your body, leading to reduced stress and anxiety.

3.   Enhances Enjoyment: Mindful movement encourages you to enjoy the process of moving, making exercise more fulfilling.

Action Step: The 5-Minute Mindful Walk

1.   Choose Your Route: Find a safe place to walk, whether it's indoors or outdoors.
2.   Set an Intention: Before you start, set a simple intention for your walk—perhaps to appreciate nature or to focus on your breath.
3.   Walk Slowly: Begin walking at a slower pace than usual. Notice how your feet feel as they connect with the ground.
4.   Engage Your Senses:
•   Sight: Observe the colors and details of your surroundings. What catches your eye?
•   Sound: Listen to the sounds around you. Are there birds singing, leaves rustling, or distant voices?
•   Breath: Pay attention to your breath as you walk. Notice the rhythm and how it changes with movement.
5.   Reflect on Your Experience: After five minutes, pause and reflect on how the mindful walk affected your mood and mindset.

Example Exercise: Mindful Stretching

1.   Find a Comfortable Space: Choose a quiet area where you can stretch without distractions.
2.   Choose Simple Stretches: Focus on a few gentle stretches that feel good for your

body, like neck rolls, shoulder shrugs, or side stretches.

3. Breathe Deeply: As you stretch, coordinate your movements with your breath. Inhale as you lengthen your body, exhale as you release tension.

4. Notice Sensations: Pay close attention to how your muscles feel during each stretch. What sensations arise?

Chapter Summary

Mindful movement allows you to connect with your body and enhance your physical awareness. By practicing mindful walking and stretching, you cultivate a sense of presence and enjoyment in your physical activities, making mindfulness an integral part of your daily routine.

Chapter 5: Mindfulness in Daily Activities

Integrating Mindfulness into Everyday Life

Mindfulness isn't limited to formal practices; it can be woven into your daily activities. By bringing awareness to routine tasks, you can transform mundane moments into opportunities for mindfulness.

The Value of Mindful Living

1. Increases Presence: Mindful living encourages you to fully engage with whatever you're doing, enhancing your overall experience.
2. Reduces Stress: Bringing awareness to daily tasks helps reduce stress and anxiety by keeping you grounded in the present.

3.   Enhances Satisfaction: Focusing on the present moment can increase your enjoyment of everyday activities.

Action Step: Mindfulness During Routine Tasks

1.   Choose a Daily Task: Pick a task you perform regularly, such as washing dishes, brushing your teeth, or commuting.
2.   Set an Intention: Before you begin, set an intention to practice mindfulness during this task.
3.   Engage Fully:
• Notice Sensations: Pay attention to the physical sensations involved in the task. How does the water feel on your hands? What sounds do you hear?
• Stay Present: If your mind wanders, gently bring it back to the task at hand. Acknowledge any distractions without judgment.
4.   Reflect on the Experience: After completing the task, take a moment to reflect on how mindfulness changed your experience. Did you feel more relaxed or connected to the moment?

Example Exercise: Mindful Eating (Expanded)

1.   Prepare Your Meal: As you cook, focus on the colours, textures, and smells of the ingredients. Be present in the process.
2.   Savor Each Bite: When eating, take a moment to appreciate the appearance of your food before tasting it.

3. Chew Slowly: Focus on the flavors and textures as you chew, putting down your fork between bites to fully engage with your food.

4. Express Gratitude: Before finishing, take a moment to express gratitude for the meal and the effort that went into preparing it.

Chapter Summary

Integrating mindfulness into daily activities enhances your overall experience and fosters a greater sense of presence in your life. By practicing mindfulness during routine tasks, you can transform mundane moments into opportunities for reflection and calm.

Chapter 6: Mindfulness and Technology

Navigating a Digital World Mindfully

In today's fast-paced, technology-driven society, it's easy to get lost in the sea of notifications, emails, and social media. Mindfulness can help you regain control and navigate technology in a way that enhances rather than detracts from your well-being.

The Impact of Technology on Mindfulness

1. Increases Distraction: Constant notifications and digital clutter can pull your attention away from the present moment.
2. Reduces Connection: Over-reliance on technology can diminish face-to-face interactions and create a sense of isolation.

3. Encourages Mindlessness: Scrolling through social media or binge-watching shows can lead to mindless consumption rather than meaningful engagement.

Action Step: Conduct a Mindful Tech Audit

1. Assess Your Digital Habits: Take 10 minutes to reflect on how you use technology daily. What apps do you spend the most time on? How does your technology use make you feel?
2. Set Intentions: Decide which technologies enhance your life and which may be distractions. For example, social media might connect you with friends but can also lead to comparison and dissatisfaction.
3. Limit Notifications: Turn off non-essential notifications on your devices. This reduces distractions and helps you engage more fully with what matters.
4. Establish Tech-Free Zones: Create spaces in your home where technology is not allowed, such as the dining room or bedroom, to promote more meaningful connections and relaxation.

Example Exercise: Mindful Social Media Use

1. Set Boundaries: Decide on specific times for checking social media rather than scrolling mindlessly throughout the day.
2. Curate Your Feed: Unfollow accounts that do not inspire or uplift you. Surround yourself with positive content that aligns with your values.

3. Engage Intentionally: When using social media, take a moment to engage mindfully. Comment, share, or react thoughtfully, rather than scrolling through posts passively.

Chapter Summary

Mindfulness can help you navigate technology in a way that enhances your life. By conducting a mindful tech audit and establishing boundaries, you can reclaim your time and attention, ensuring that technology serves you rather than distracts you.

Chapter 7: The Power of Gratitude in Mindfulness

Cultivating a Gratitude Mindset

Gratitude is a powerful aspect of mindfulness that shifts your focus from what you lack to what you have. Practicing gratitude enhances your overall well-being and fosters a more positive outlook on life.

The Benefits of Gratitude

1. Boosts Happiness: Regularly acknowledging what you're thankful for can increase your overall sense of happiness and contentment.
2. Reduces Negative Emotions: Gratitude can counteract feelings of envy, resentment, and regret.

3.   Enhances Relationships: Expressing gratitude strengthens social bonds and fosters a sense of connection with others.

Action Step: Daily Gratitude Practice

1.   Set Aside Time: Choose a specific time each day, such as morning or before bed, to reflect on what you're grateful for.
2.   Keep a Gratitude Journal: Write down three things you're grateful for each day. They can be small (a good cup of coffee) or significant (supportive friends).
3.   Reflect on Your Entries: Take a moment to reflect on how each item on your list makes you feel. Why are you grateful for it? How does it impact your life?

Example Exercise: Gratitude Letters

1.   Choose Someone Special: Think of someone who has made a positive impact on your life—this could be a friend, family member, or mentor.
2.   Write a Letter: Take the time to write a letter expressing your gratitude. Be specific about what they did and how it affected you.
3.   Share Your Letter: If possible, deliver the letter in person or read it to them. This not only strengthens your relationship but also reinforces your own feelings of gratitude.

Chapter Summary

Cultivating a gratitude mindset enhances your mindfulness practice and improves your overall well-being. By incorporating a daily gratitude practice and expressing appreciation to others, you create a positive feedback loop that fosters happiness and connection.

Chapter 8: Creating Your Mindfulness Routine

Establishing a Consistent Mindfulness Practice

Creating a mindfulness routine helps you integrate mindfulness into your daily life seamlessly. Consistency is key to reaping the benefits of mindfulness, allowing you to cultivate a greater sense of awareness and calm.

Elements of an Effective Mindfulness Routine

1. Set Clear Goals: Identify what you want to achieve through mindfulness. This could be reducing stress, enhancing focus, or fostering a sense of peace.

2. Choose Your Practices: Select a variety of mindfulness practices that resonate with you, such as breath awareness, mindful observation, or gratitude journaling.
3. Create a Schedule: Set aside specific times each day for your mindfulness practice. Consistency helps reinforce the habit.

Action Step: Design Your Mindfulness Routine

1. Morning Mindfulness: Start your day with a short mindfulness practice. This could be five minutes of focused breathing or a gratitude exercise.
2. Midday Check-in: Take a moment during your lunch break to pause and engage in mindful observation or a brief walk.
3. Evening Reflection: End your day by journaling about your experiences, focusing on moments of mindfulness or gratitude.

Example Routine:

- Morning (5 minutes): Practice the 4-7-8 breathing technique.
- Midday (5 minutes): Engage in mindful movement with a brief walk.
- Evening (10 minutes): Reflect on your day and write in your gratitude journal.

Chapter Summary

Establishing a mindfulness routine enhances your practice and integrates mindfulness into your life. By setting clear goals, choosing your practices, and creating a schedule, you can cultivate a consistent mindfulness practice that yields lasting benefits.

Chapter 9: Mindfulness in Everyday Activities

Bringing Mindfulness to Daily Tasks

Mindfulness doesn't have to be confined to a meditation cushion. You can incorporate it into everyday activities, transforming mundane tasks into opportunities for awareness and presence.

Finding Mindfulness in Routine Tasks

1. Eating Mindfully: Turn meals into mindful experiences by savouring each bite. Pay attention to the flavour's, textures, and aromas of your food. Chew slowly and notice how the food nourishes your body.
2. Mindful Commuting: Whether you're driving, biking, or taking public transport, use this time to practice

mindfulness. Focus on your breathing, observe your surroundings, or listen to a guided meditation or calming music.

3. Cleaning Mindfully: Transform chores into a mindful practice by focusing entirely on the task at hand. Notice the sensations of scrubbing, the smell of cleaning products, and the satisfaction of a tidy space.

Action Step: Mindful Activity Challenge

1. Choose a Daily Activity: Pick a routine task, such as washing dishes, brushing your teeth, or folding laundry.
2. Engage Fully: During this activity, concentrate on each movement, sensation, and sound. If your mind wanders, gently bring your focus back to the task.
3. Reflect: After completing the task, take a moment to reflect on the experience. How did it feel to be fully present? What did you notice that you usually overlook?

Example Exercise: Mindful Walking

1. Find a Quiet Space: Choose a location where you can walk without distractions, such as a park or a quiet street.
2. Focus on Your Steps: Pay attention to the sensations in your feet as they touch the ground. Notice the rhythm of your breath and how your body moves.
3. Engage Your Senses: Observe your surroundings—what do you see, hear, and smell? Let the experience of walking become a meditative practice.

Chapter Summary

Incorporating mindfulness into daily activities enhances your ability to stay present and engaged. By transforming routine tasks into mindful experiences, you cultivate awareness and appreciation for the moment, enriching your life.

Chapter 10: Overcoming Mindfulness Challenges

Navigating Common Obstacles

While mindfulness can be a powerful tool, it's not always easy to practice. Recognizing and addressing common challenges can help you maintain your mindfulness journey.

Identifying Challenges to Mindfulness

1. Distractions: External distractions, such as noise or interruptions, can hinder your practice. Internal distractions, like racing thoughts, can also pull you away from the present moment.
2. Impatience: Mindfulness is a skill that takes time to develop. You might feel

frustrated if you don't notice immediate benefits.

3. Self-Criticism: Many people struggle with self-doubt and judgment during mindfulness practice. This can create resistance and diminish your ability to be present.

Action Step: Develop Strategies for Overcoming Obstacles

1. Create a Distraction-Free Zone: Designate a specific area for your mindfulness practice, free from noise and interruptions. This could be a corner of your room, a quiet park, or even your office.
2. Practice Self-Compassion: Acknowledge that mindfulness is a journey. It's okay if your mind wanders or if you struggle to focus. Treat yourself with kindness and patience.
3. Set Realistic Expectations: Remember that mindfulness is not about achieving perfection. Aim for progress over perfection and celebrate small wins.

Example Exercise: Mindfulness and Distraction

1. Identify Your Distractions: Take 5 minutes to jot down common distractions that pull you away from mindfulness. This could include notifications, noise, or racing thoughts.
2. Create a Plan: Develop strategies to mitigate these distractions. For example, silence your phone during practice or use

noise-cancelling headphones to reduce external noise.

3. Revisit and Adjust: Regularly reassess your mindfulness practice. Are there new distractions? How can you adapt to maintain your focus?

Chapter Summary

Overcoming challenges in mindfulness requires self-awareness and proactive strategies. By creating a distraction-free zone, practicing self-compassion, and setting realistic expectations, you can navigate obstacles and deepen your mindfulness practice.

Chapter 11: Mindfulness for Stress Management

Using Mindfulness to Alleviate Stress

Mindfulness can be a powerful ally in managing stress. By developing awareness and acceptance, you can reduce anxiety and enhance your ability to cope with life's challenges.

Understanding Stress Responses

1. Physical Reactions: Stress triggers physical responses in your body, such as increased heart rate, muscle tension, and shallow breathing.
2. Emotional Impact: Stress can lead to feelings of overwhelm, irritability, and sadness, affecting your overall well-being.
3. Cognitive Effects: High levels of stress can impair your ability to think clearly, make decisions, and concentrate.

Action Step: Mindfulness Techniques for Stress Relief

1. Breath Awareness: When stress arises, take a moment to focus on your breath. Inhale deeply through your nose for a count of four, hold for a count of four, and exhale through your mouth for a count of six. Repeat several times to center yourself.

2. Body Scan: Perform a quick body scan to release tension. Close your eyes, take a deep breath, and mentally check in with each part of your body, relaxing any areas of tightness.

3. Nature Breaks: Spend a few minutes in nature, whether it's a walk in the park or sitting outside. Notice the sights, sounds, and smells around you, allowing nature to ground you.

Example Exercise: Stress Journal

1. Keep a Journal: Write down your stress triggers and how they make you feel. Reflect on patterns or recurring themes.

2. Explore Mindfulness Responses: For each trigger, write down a mindful response you can use. For example, if you feel stressed about work deadlines, your response might be to practice breath awareness before starting tasks.

3. Review Regularly: Set aside time each week to review your journal. Notice any shifts in your stress levels and the effectiveness of your mindfulness strategies.

Chapter Summary

Mindfulness is a valuable tool for managing stress and enhancing your ability to cope with challenges. By practicing breath awareness, body scans, and connecting with nature, you can cultivate a sense of calm amidst life's pressures.

Chapter 12: Integrating Mindfulness into Your Lifestyle

Making Mindfulness a Habit

To truly benefit from mindfulness, it's essential to integrate it into your lifestyle. This means making mindfulness a consistent part of your daily routine and mindset.

Creating a Mindful Lifestyle

1. Set Intentions: Each morning, set a mindful intention for the day. This could be focusing on being present, practicing gratitude, or approaching challenges with curiosity.
2. Mindful Transitions: Use transitions between activities as opportunities for

mindfulness. For example, take a moment to breathe deeply before starting a new task or entering a meeting.

3. Involve Others: Share your mindfulness journey with friends or family. Engaging others can enhance your practice and create a supportive community.

Action Step: Design Your Mindful Lifestyle

1. Daily Intentions: At the beginning of each day, write down one intention that guides your mindfulness practice. For example, "Today, I will be present in each conversation."

2. Mindful Check-ins: Set reminders throughout the day to pause and take a few mindful breaths. Use these moments to reconnect with your intention and the present moment.

3. Weekly Reflection: Dedicate time each week to reflect on your mindfulness practice. What worked well? What challenges did you face? Adjust your approach as needed.

Example Exercise: Mindful Planning

1. Plan Mindfully: When planning your week, consider how to incorporate mindfulness practices into your schedule. Identify specific times for practice and set goals for each day.

2. Engage in Mindful Activities: Choose activities that align with your mindfulness goals, such as yoga, nature walks, or meditation.

3.   Invite Others: Plan mindful activities with friends or family to enhance your experience and build connections.

Chapter Summary

Integrating mindfulness into your lifestyle creates lasting change and enhances your well-being. By setting daily intentions, using mindful transitions, and involving others in your practice, you cultivate a mindful mindset that permeates every aspect of your life.

Conclusion: Your Mindful Journey Begins Now

Congratulations on reaching the end of "Mindfulness in 5 Minutes." You've equipped yourself with practical tools and strategies to cultivate mindfulness in your daily life. Remember, mindfulness is not a destination but a journey—one that unfolds with each moment you choose to be present.

Actionable Challenge: Start Today

As you close this book, I encourage you to take immediate action. Reflect on the techniques you've learned and choose one to implement right now. Perhaps it's a quick breathing exercise, a mindful walk, or simply pausing to savor your next meal.

Leave Behind the Overwhelm

The world is filled with distractions and noise, but you have the power to carve out moments of peace and clarity. Make a commitment to yourself: dedicate just five minutes a day to practice mindfulness. This small step can lead to significant changes in your mental and emotional well-being.

What's Your Next Mindful Moment?

Ask yourself: What will I do in the next five minutes to practice mindfulness? Whether it's sitting in silence, observing nature, or focusing on your breath, take that action. Embrace the present, and let mindfulness guide you toward a more peaceful and fulfilling life.

Your journey starts now.

Be Mindful, Be Present & Thrive.

Mindfulness in 5 minutes   Micro Series

www.ingramcontent.com/pod-product-compliance
Lightning Source LLC
Chambersburg PA
CBHW030517220526
45464CB00006B/2830